S0-AJA-974

HEAT

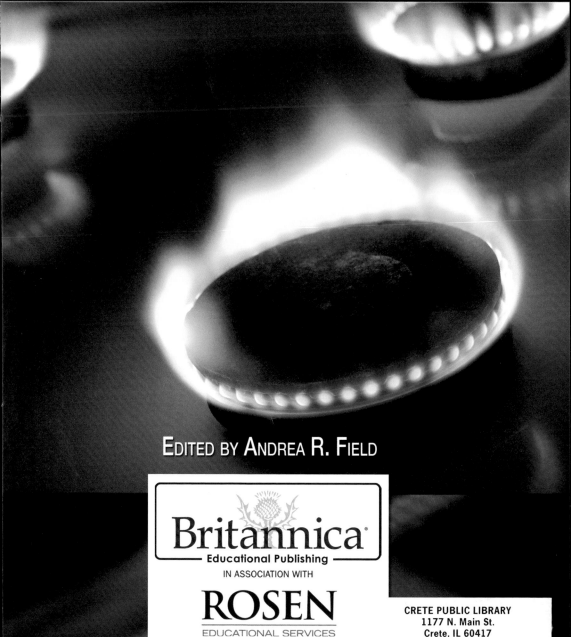

EDITED BY ANDREA R. FIELD

Britannica
Educational Publishing
IN ASSOCIATION WITH

ROSEN
EDUCATIONAL SERVICES

CRETE PUBLIC LIBRARY
1177 N. Main St.
Crete, IL 60417

Published in 2013 by Britannica Educational Publishing
(a trademark of Encyclopædia Britannica, Inc.)
in association with Rosen Educational Services, LLC
29 East 21st Street, New York, NY 10010.

Copyright © 2013 Encyclopædia Britannica, Inc. Britannica, Encyclopædia Britannica, and the
Thistle logo are registered trademarks of Encyclopædia Britannica, Inc. All rights reserved.

Rosen Educational Services materials copyright © 2013 Rosen Educational Services, LLC.
All rights reserved.

Distributed exclusively by Rosen Educational Services.
For a listing of additional Britannica Educational Publishing titles, call toll free (800) 237-9932.

First Edition

Britannica Educational Publishing
J.E. Luebering: Director, Core Reference Group, Encyclopædia Britannica
Adam Augustyn: Assistant Manager, Encyclopædia Britannica

Anthony L. Green: Editor, Compton's by Britannica
Michael Anderson: Senior Editor, Compton's by Britannica
Andrea R. Field: Senior Editor, Compton's by Britannica
Sherman Hollar: Associate Editor, Compton's by Britannica

Marilyn L. Barton: Senior Coordinator, Production Control
Steven Bosco: Director, Editorial Technologies
Lisa S. Braucher: Senior Producer and Data Editor
Yvette Charboneau: Senior Copy Editor
Kathy Nakamura: Manager, Media Acquisition

Rosen Educational Services
Shalini Saxena: Editor
Nelson Sá: Art Director
Cindy Reiman: Photography Manager
Karen Huang: Photo Researcher
Brian Garvey: Designer, Cover Design
Introduction by Shalini Saxena

Library of Congress Cataloging-in-Publication Data

Heat/edited by Andrea R. Field.
    p. cm.—(Introduction to physics)
"In association with Britannica Educational Publishing, Rosen Educational Services."
Includes bibliographical references and index.
ISBN 978-1-61530-838-5 (library binding)
1. Heat—Juvenile literature. I. Field, Andrea R.
QC256.H436 2013
536—dc23

2011053232

Manufactured in the United States of America

Cover (burner), p. 3: ccat82/Shutterstock.com; cover (equation) EtiAmmos/Shutterstock.com; pp. 10,
20, 30, 38, 50, 65, 67, 70, 73, 74 © iStockphoto.com/Milos Jokic; remaining interior background images
© iStockphoto.com/Floriana Barbu

J
536
HEA

CONTENTS

3 1886 00196 8762

The sting we feel after touching a hot pan, the welcome relief of a cold drink on a warm day, and the comfort of a heater as it thaws our frozen limbs are sensations that are familiar to most of us—indeed, hotness and coldness texture a number of our everyday experiences. We may throw around terms such as "heat" and "temperature" casually in conversation to describe what we perceive in such situations, but physics shows us that these are not interchangeable terms. As you will discover in these pages, we must begin at the atomic level of matter to understand heat and the related concepts of temperature and thermal energy as well as the relationships between them.

In physics the term "heat" refers to the energy that is transferred from a warmer object to a colder one. The energy that is transferred must, of course, come from somewhere. In fact, it all starts with the atoms and molecules that compose all matter. Each of these particles is constantly moving and generating energy from this motion. This is called kinetic energy. The total amount of kinetic energy an object has is equal to its thermal energy—that is, the energy that an object has stored as a result of its temperature. To illustrate, let's consider a pot of soup and a cup of soup ladled from it. The thermal energy of the pot is greater because it has more particles that are moving and creating energy.

Temperature represents the average speed of all the particles in an object: the faster its particles move, the higher its temperature will be. Unlike thermal energy, temperature does not depend on the quantity of the substance. In the case of the pot and cup of soup, the average speed of the particles may be the same in both, thus giving them the same temperature even though they differ in size.

In most instances, when heat is transferred from a warmer substance to a colder one, the temperature of the warmer substance will decrease while that of the colder one will increase. This will continue until the two are at the same temperature. At other times, however, heat transfer may not cause a change in temperature at all; rather, the molecules of the heat-absorbing substance may change and rearrange themselves in what is called a phase change. One example of this is the change of water to vapor as it is heated.

Both temperature and heat can be measured. The Fahrenheit and Celsius scales, named after Daniel Gabriel Fahrenheit and Anders Celsius, respectively, are perhaps the most commonly known and are frequently used on temperature-measuring instruments called thermometers. Heat changes in a physical or chemical reaction can be measured with a device called a calorimeter.

Anders Celsius, for whom the Celsius temperature scale is named.
Science Source/Photo Researchers, Inc.

The process of heat transfer can occur through a few different methods. Conduction is heat transfer between adjacent parts of a body or through direct contact between two bodies. Convection transfers heat by movement of a heated fluid such as air or water. In contrast, heat transfer through radiation requires neither contact nor a medium to carry the energy. In this process, energy is emitted (radiated) by a heated surface and travels to another surface, where it is absorbed. Heat transfer usually involves some combination of all three of these processes.

The relationships between heat, other forms of energy, temperature, and work form the basis of thermodynamics. The three basic laws of thermodynamics describe the nature of these relationships and hold true for all biological and physical systems. Indeed, much of our understanding of the universe is informed in part by thermodynamics.

Although we may only think about heat incidentally, heat is always around us in one form or another. It is critical to all life, and our ability to tackle issues in such areas as climate change, biology, and technology rests on our application of the fundamental concepts you will encounter in this book.

CHAPTER 1

WHAT IS HEAT?

Heat is so well known from our earliest childhood that we hardly think about it. A steaming bowl of soup, an active radiator, and a sauna feel hot; a book and a chocolate bar at room temperature seem less hot; and an ice cube feels cold. In everyday speech it is common to say that the soup has more heat than the book and that the ice cube has less heat than the chocolate bar. However, people often use the word "heat" when what they really mean is temperature or a type of energy called thermal energy.

Temperature is a measure of hotness or coldness. In physics, heat refers specifically to energy that is transferred from one thing to another because of a difference in temperature. If two objects at different temperatures are brought together, energy is transferred— that is, heat flows—from the hotter object to the colder one. A radiator gives off heat, warming the cooler air around it. If a person holds an unwrapped chocolate bar, his or her hands transmit heat to the chocolate, eventually melting it. It is incorrect to speak of the heat in an object itself because heat is restricted to energy being transferred. Energy that is stored in an object because of its temperature is called thermal energy.

It can be difficult at first to understand the difference between heat, temperature, and thermal energy. To better understand these three related concepts, it is helpful to know what actually makes things hot or cold. Heat,

The woman's hand transmits heat to the chocolate bar—which is at a lower temperature than her hand—and causes it to melt.
© Westend61/Superstock

temperature, and thermal energy are all concerned with microscopic movements within matter. These movements are explained by what is called the kinetic theory of matter.

MOLECULES IN MOTION

All matter, whether a solid, liquid, or gas, is composed of tiny particles such as molecules and atoms. These particles are constantly in motion—traveling, vibrating, or rotating randomly in all directions. One of the many different forms of energy is the energy something has because of its motion. This type of energy is called kinetic energy. The kinetic energy of the particles in matter is the basis of temperature, thermal energy, and heat.

Temperature is the measurement of how fast, on average, the particles in something are moving. Microwaving a bowl of soup, for example, raises the temperature of the soup by speeding up the average motion of its molecules. The molecules in the hot soup are traveling faster overall than they did before the soup was heated. The molecules in an ice cube are moving more slowly.

Temperature is thus a measure of intensity. It does not depend on the quantity of matter being considered. An ice chip and

A diagram of an atom, with electrons orbiting a nucleus. All matter is composed of atoms, which, although invisible to the human eye, move and vibrate constantly, creating kinetic energy.
Mushakesa/Shutterstock.com

a brick of ice will have the same temperature if the average speed of their particles is the same.

Thermal energy, on the other hand, represents the total amount of kinetic energy of an object's molecules and other particles. A hot bowl of soup has more thermal energy than a cold bowl of soup because the total amount of its particles' motion is greater. However,

Although this Antarctic iceberg is cold to the touch, it has a great deal of thermal energy because of the combined motion of all of its particles. It thus has the potential to give off far more heat than a much smaller bowl of soup, even if the soup feels piping hot. **Volodymyr Goinyk/Shutterstock.com**

a hot bowl of soup possesses more thermal energy than a cup of soup at the same temperature. Likewise, an iceberg has far more thermal energy than a piping-hot bowl of soup. The iceberg is so much larger than the bowl of soup that the sum of the motion of all its particles is greater than that of the soup. This is true even though the soup has a higher temperature. Temperature is a measure of the overall speed of the particles' motion; thermal energy, of the total energy they have because of their motion.

Thermal energy represents the amount of heat that something could potentially give off. Heat is the transfer of thermal energy from a hotter substance to a colder one. Transferring heat to a substance usually raises its temperature.

ACHIEVING BALANCE

If a hot poker is plunged into cold water, the poker becomes cooler and the water becomes warmer. This means that the hot body gives up some of its heat to the cold body. The molecules in the water speed up, and the water gains energy; at the same time those in the poker slow down, and the poker loses energy. The exchange of heat will continue

EXPANSION AND CONTRACTION

In nearly all cases, matter increases in volume when there is an increase in temperature. In gases the increase is a large one. As the molecules that make up the gas begin speeding up, they also begin spreading out. If the pressure and weight of the gas remain the same, the increase in volume will be in direct proportion to the increase in temperature.

The transfer of heat to a solid causes it to expand also but to a much smaller degree than a gas. In a metal rod every unit length of the rod becomes longer when it expands. Liquids in general behave like solids and expand slightly when the temperature is raised.

The reverse is also true: when an object gives off heat and its temperature drops, it contracts.

Metal rods, such as these, expand and become longer when heated. **Jeremy Hoare/Life File/ Photodisc/Getty Images**

until the water and the poker have the same temperature. This balance in temperatures is known as thermal equilibrium. Likewise, if a metal spoon at room temperature is put into a cup of hot tea, the tea transmits heat to the spoon, raising the temperature of the spoon while its own temperature decreases. The tea will continue to transfer heat until it is the same temperature as the spoon. Thus the

Heat always flows from a warmer substance to a colder one. In a glass of water with ice where the water is at a higher temperature than the ice, heat flows from the water, causing the ice to melt. **DAJ/ Getty Images**

temperature of an object determines whether heat flows from it or to it when it is in contact with another object at a different temperature.

Heat always flows naturally from the hotter substance to the colder one; it can never flow spontaneously from a colder object to a hotter one. If a film showed a glass of warm water changing on its own into a glass of hot water with ice floating on top, it would immediately be obvious that the film was running backward.

PHASE CHANGES

When a hotter substance transfers heat to a colder one, the effect is usually to raise the temperature of the colder substance. This is most often, but not always, the case. A substance may absorb heat without an increase in temperature by changing from one physical state, or phase — solid, liquid, or gas — to another. For example, a solid can change to a liquid by melting, or it can transform directly into a gas by a process known as sublimation. Likewise, a liquid can change into a gas by boiling.

In these cases, the heat transfer causes the particles of the substance to rearrange themselves, rather than to speed up. The increased energy is used to overcome the forces that hold together the atoms or molecules in a material. The particles in a solid are bound together more tightly than those in a liquid, for instance. If an ice cube (solid water) is placed on a countertop, heat is transferred from the surrounding air to the ice. While the ice melts, the heat transfer does not change the temperature of the ice. The heat instead causes the molecules to spread out more, transforming the ice into a liquid. The melting ice remains at 32° F (0° C), and the liquid water that is formed is also at 32° F. Once the ice has melted, the temperature of the liquid water will then start to rise.

The amount of energy absorbed or released by a substance during a phase change is known as latent heat. This energy transfer occurs without a change in temperature. The transfer of energy that causes a change of temperature but not a change of phase is known as sensible heat.

When water is boiled on a stove, it undergoes a phase change—or a change in physical state—from liquid to gas without experiencing a change in temperature. Shane Trotter/Shutterstock.com

CHAPTER 2

MEASURING TEMPERATURE

T emperature is expressed as degrees in terms of an arbitrary scale. There are three such scales in general use: Fahrenheit, Celsius, and Kelvin.

TEMPERATURE SCALES

To measure temperature exactly it is necessary to design and construct a thermometer scale. There are two types of thermometer scale, one based on two fixed points and one called an absolute temperature scale.

FAHRENHEIT AND CELSIUS

In one type of temperature scale, two natural events, each of which always occurs at the same temperature, are selected. The freezing point of water and the boiling point of water are two such fixed points that can be reproduced easily. Then a number that indicates a temperature is arbitrarily assigned to each of these fixed points. Finally the interval

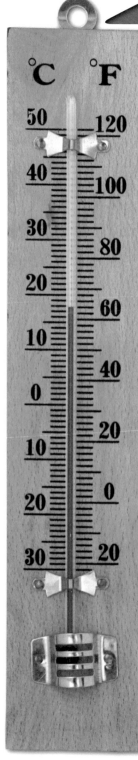

between these points is divided into a fixed number of equal degrees. A temperature below zero is marked negative.

Two temperature scales based on the fixed points of boiling water and freezing water are in general use. The Fahrenheit (° F) scale is used in the United States and a few other English-speaking countries. It assigns 32° F for the freezing point of water and 212° F for the boiling point of water. The interval between the two is divided into 180 equal degrees. This scale was devised, in an earlier form, by the 18th-century German physicist Daniel Gabriel Fahrenheit.

Many liquid thermometers show temperature on both the Celsius and Fahrenheit scales. **Dvirus/ Shutterstock.com**

The Celsius (° C) scale is widely used for scientific measurement. It is also in everyday use in much of the world, in countries where the metric system has been adopted. In this scale 0° C is the freezing point of water and 100° C is the boiling point of water. The interval between them is divided into 100 degrees. The scale was invented in 1742 by the Swedish astronomer Anders Celsius. It has sometimes also been called the centigrade scale.

KELVIN

The Celsius and Fahrenheit scales each have a corresponding absolute temperature scale. Many physical laws and scientific formulas can be expressed more simply when an absolute temperature scale is used. In such a scale, zero degrees is equal to absolute zero, the coldest temperature that is theoretically possible. At absolute zero the particles of a substance have the lowest possible energy. Because absolute scales set their zero point at this lowest possible temperature, they have no negative values.

The absolute scale based on Celsius is called the Kelvin (K) scale, after the 19th-century British physicist Lord Kelvin. The Kelvin scale has been adopted as the

British physicist William Thomson, who was later known as Lord Kelvin. FPG/Archive Photos/Getty Images

international standard for scientific temperature measurement. Because absolute zero is equal to -273.15° C on the Celsius scale, the Kelvin scale is essentially the Celsius scale shifted by 273.15 degrees. The unit of temperature in the Kelvin scale is the kelvin, and it is equal in size to the Celsius degree. The degree symbol is not used with values on the Kelvin scale, so the boiling point of water is expressed as 373.15 K (not 373.15° K).

The absolute scale based on Fahrenheit is called the Rankine scale. It was once used in certain engineering fields in the United States.

It is often necessary to convert a temperature on one scale to a corresponding temperature on another. The basic conversion factors are as follows.

Fahrenheit to Celsius: $°C = (°F - 32) \div 1.8$

Celsius to Fahrenheit: $°F = (°C \times 1.8) + 32$

Celsius to Kelvin: $K = °C + 273.15$

THERMOMETERS

Temperature is measured by an instrument called a thermometer. The invention of the

ABSOLUTE ZERO:
HOW LOW CAN YOU GO?

If temperature is a measurement of how fast overall the particles in a substance are moving, there must be a minimum temperature at which the particles stop moving. This temperature is known as absolute zero, and it is extremely low: -459.67° F (-273.15° C). Actually, at absolute zero the particles would not stop moving completely but very nearly so. Their motion would be the least amount possible. With such minimal thermal energy, the substance would not be able to transfer any heat.

7.3′

Although no substance can reach absolute zero, extremely low temperatures can be maintained using a device called a cryostat, such as this one, which was used to keep the temperature of NASA's Cosmic Background Explorer (COBE) satellite low enough that it could function. **Science & Society Picture Library/Getty Images**

Absolute zero is the lowest temperature that could theoretically exist. In reality, no substance can ever become that cold, though it can approach that temperature closely. Scientists have cooled materials to less than a billionth of a degree above absolute zero. At such temperatures the thermal, electric, and magnetic properties of many substances undergo great changes. Indeed, the behavior of matter cooled to that extent seems strange when compared with that at room temperature. For instance, some solids show no resistance whatsoever to the flow of electricity. When liquid helium approaches absolute zero, it can flow through tiny holes impervious to any other liquid.

thermometer is generally credited to the Italian mathematician and physicist Galileo. In his instrument, built in about 1592, the changing temperature of an inverted glass vessel produced an expansion or contraction of the air within it. This in turn changed the level of a liquid inside the vessel's long, open-mouthed neck.

Any substance that somehow changes with alterations in its temperature can be

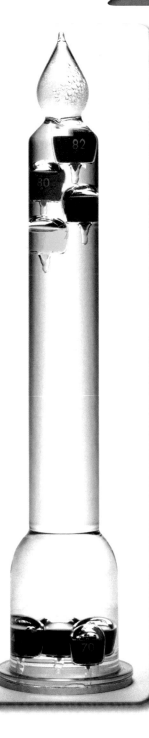

used as the basic component in a thermometer. Gas thermometers work best at very low temperatures. Liquid thermometers are more common. They are simple, inexpensive, long-lasting, and able to measure a wide temperature span.

The liquid is almost always mercury, sealed in a glass tube with nitrogen gas making up the rest of the volume of the tube. If the mercury is heated up, it expands, and if it is cooled, it contracts. This change produces a noticeable rise or fall in the mercury level in the tube. Markings on the outside of the tube indicate the corresponding rise or fall in degrees according to a temperature scale.

Electronic digital thermometers operate on the

A replica of Galileo's thermometer. Science & Society Picture Library/Getty Images principle that electrical resistance in a metal (usually platinum) varies with changes in temperature. Electricity flows more easily through a platinum wire when the wire's

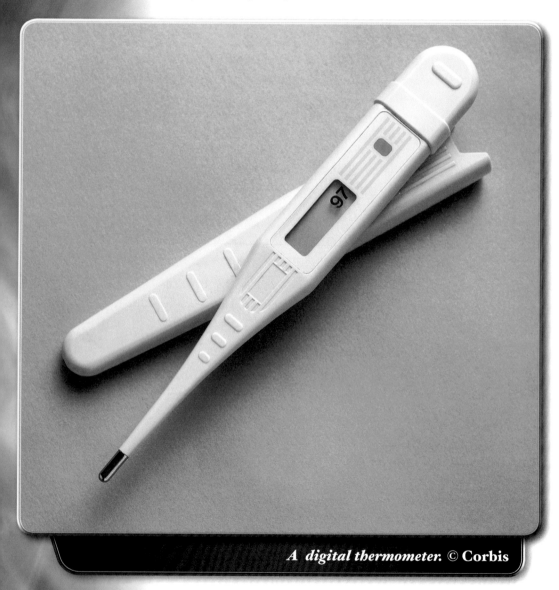

A digital thermometer. © **Corbis**

temperature decreases. When the thermometer is in use, a voltage is applied, causing an electric current to flow through the platinum wire. The measure of this current is an indication of the resistance—and thus the temperature—of the wire. A computer chip measures the current, calculates the temperature, and displays it on a screen.

Thermocouples are among the most widely used industrial thermometers. They are composed of two wires made of different materials. The wires are joined together at both ends and connected to a voltage-measuring device. One end of the joined wires is placed where the temperature is to be measured, and the other is kept at a constant lower temperature. The temperature difference between the two ends creates a voltage that can be measured and translated into a measure of the temperature.

CHAPTER 3

MEASURING HEAT

A ll of the many forms of energy, including heat, can be converted into work.
For this reason, amounts of energy
are expressed in units of work. To measure the
amount of heat transferred during a chemical or physical reaction, the most commonly

Equipment in a laboratory. When a chemical reaction takes place, heat is often released and can be measured. **Jupiterimages/ Comstock/Thinkstock**

used units are the calorie, the joule, and the British thermal unit.

SPECIFIC HEAT

In the 18th century the Scottish scientist Joseph Black noticed that equal masses of different substances needed different amounts of heat transferred to raise their temperature by the same amount. For example, it takes far more heat to raise the temperature of a gram of water by one degree than it does to raise a gram of mercury by one degree. From his observations, Black founded the concept of specific heat. The specific heat of a substance is the amount of energy required to raise a unit mass of a substance through a specified temperature interval, usually one degree. The value for specific heat varies widely for different substances.

In the metric system the unit of specific heat is the calorie. It is defined as the amount of heat that is required to raise the temperature of one gram of water from $14.5°$ C to $15.5°$ C. The specific heat of water is set at 1.000 calorie per gram. All other values are based on this unit. (The calorie used to measure specific heat is not the same as the unit used in

Drops of mercury. Mercury has a lower specific heat than water and is often used in liquid thermometers. Cordelia Molloy/ Science Photo Library/Getty Images

nutrition. The "calorie" used to measure how much energy the body can get from foods is actually the kilocalorie, which is equal to 1,000 calories.)

Specific heat can also be expressed in joules, a unit of work or energy in the International System of Units (SI). One calorie is equal to 4.1855 joules.

In the English system of measurements the British thermal unit (BTU) is the unit of specific heat. One British thermal unit is the amount of heat required to raise the temperature of one pound of water from 63° F to 64° F. One BTU is equal to about 252 calories. In measuring the heat content of fuels the British thermal unit is the unit of specific heat used.

MEASURING HEAT TRANSFER

In a chemical or physical reaction, the amount of heat transferred is the quantity of heat that is absorbed or lost by the surroundings. Q is the symbol for the quantity of this heat transfer. If heat is lost, Q is a positive number and the reaction is called exothermic. If heat is absorbed, Q is a negative number and the reaction is called endothermic.

The amount of heat transferred can be measured with an instrument called a calorimeter. Basically, a calorimeter consists of a vessel placed in a larger vessel that is filled with a liquid such as water. The smaller vessel is where the reaction takes place. The water in the larger vessel absorbs the heat of the reaction and increases in temperature.

JOSEPH BLACK

The Scottish chemist and physicist Joseph Black (1728–99) made lasting contributions to the study of heat. He not only developed the concept of specific heat but also that of latent heat (the heat involved in a phase change, such as freezing, melting, or boiling). In addition, he made the important distinction between heat and temperature. In chemistry, he discovered the bicarbonates (such as bicarbonate of soda). Through experiments identifying carbon dioxide, which he called "fixed air," he became the first person to show that gases could be chemical substances in themselves. It had previously been thought that gases were atmospheric air in different states of purity.

Black lived and worked within the context of the Scottish Enlightenment, a remarkable flourishing of intellectual life in Scotland during the second half of the 18th century. He could count among his friends the philosopher David Hume, the economist Adam Smith, and the geologist James Hutton. While living in Glasgow, Black befriended the Scottish inventor James Watt, who was employed as instrument maker to the university there. Watt worked on developing improvements to the steam engine. His double-cylinder steam engine essentially recognized the phenomena of latent heat that Black had described.

Joseph Black visiting James Watt in his University of Glasgow workshop. © Photos.com/ Jupiterimages

Black died a celebrated death, being found by his servant with a cup of milk balanced between his knees, not a drop having been spilled. It was commented upon that this reflected the perfection of his experimental procedures.

A calorimeter used by physicist James P. Joule.
Science & Society Picture Library/Getty Images

To measure heat transfer, a mass of the substance under test is completely burned in the smaller vessel. The rise in the temperature of the water is then measured with a sensitive thermometer. Since the amount of water and the rise in temperature are known, the amount of the heat flow can be calculated. The amount of heat transferred (Q) is equal to the change in temperature of the water times the specific heat of the substance times the mass of the substance.

CHAPTER 4

How Heat Is Transferred

Heat can be transmitted by three different methods: conduction, convection, and radiation. Whether in heating a building or a kettle of water or in a natural condition such as a thunderstorm, heat transfer usually involves all these processes.

Conduction

Conduction transfers heat within a body or between two bodies that are touching. It is a point-by-point process of heat transfer. Conduction occurs in solids, liquids, or gases that are at rest. Energy flows, but the substance through which the heat is being transferred does not itself flow.

If one part of a body is heated by direct contact with a source of heat, the neighboring parts become heated successively. Thus, if a metal rod is placed in a burner, heat travels along the rod by conduction. This may be

Three Methods of Heat Transfer

1. conduction

2. convection

3. radiation

(Top) *Heat flows from the hot end to the cool end of the rod. As the distance from the burner flame increases, the temperature of the rod falls by a proportional amount. In a tea kettle (bottom left), hot water rises and cold water descends until all the water is at the same temperature. A home heating lamp (bottom right) produces its heating effect by direct transfer of radiant energy.* Encyclopædia Britannica, Inc.

explained by the kinetic theory of matter. The molecules of the rod increase their energy of motion when heated; this greater motion is then passed along the rod from molecule to molecule. Likewise, if hot soup is ladled into a room-temperature bowl, contact with the hot soup causes the molecules of the bowl to speed up, and the bowl heats up.

Conduction accounts for the transfer of heat from hot soup to the lower-temperature bowl into which it is poured.
© www.istockphoto.com/webphotographeer

Conduction involves the transfer of energy between adjacent molecules and other particles. As a particle begins to travel or vibrate more vigorously, it is more likely to collide with a neighboring particle. Such a collision knocks the neighboring particle into greater motion. It in turn is more likely to bump into other particles. In this way, greater motion is transmitted "down the line." In the case of the soup, for instance, the rapidly moving particles of hot soup that are in contact with the bowl begin to collide with the inside of the bowl. The particles of the inside of the bowl then start to move more quickly, thus colliding with particles farther inside the bowl. Heat is transferred, and the bowl's temperature rises.

CONVECTION

The method of heat transfer called convection occurs in fluids—that is, liquids and gases. It is usually a fairly rapid process and depends upon the movement of the material that is heated. The motion is a result of changes in density that accompany the heating process. Water in a tea kettle is heated by convection. A stove also heats the air in a room by convection.

THE RATE OF CONDUCTION

Conduction is usually a relatively slow process. The temperature difference between the substances and the amount and type of material involved affect the rate of heat transfer. Heat flows more quickly between substances with a greater difference in temperature. Touching a metal rod at 150° F (66° C) will heat a person's hands much faster than touching a rod that is only 100° F (38° C). As a hotter object heats up a colder one, it generally becomes cooler itself. The temperature difference between the two decreases, and the rate of heat transfer slows down.

The size and shape of the object are also factors. Heat is transferred faster through a shorter, thinner rod than through a longer, thicker one. This is because it does not have to travel as far in the shorter, thinner rod. If a bowl of soup is filled halfway, the liquid will take longer to heat up the entire bowl than if it were filled to the top. The greater the surface area of the hot soup in contact with the bowl, the faster the bowl will heat up.

Because of their atomic structure, some materials are much better conductors of heat than others. Metals are especially good conductors. If a metal spoon and a wooden spoon are placed in a pot of tomato sauce being heated on a stove, the handle of the metal spoon will heat up much faster than that of the wooden one. Air, on the other hand, is a poor conductor of heat. Gases generally have the lowest thermal conductivity, followed by liquids. Solids are the best conductors of heat.

Size and shape affect the rate at which heat is transferred. Metal rods that are thinner and shorter conduct heat faster than those that are thicker and longer. **Dusan Zidar/Shutterstock.com**

Both conduction and convection play a role in heat transfer in water being heated on a stove. Conduction warms water in contact with the bottom of the kettle. Then, through natural convection, the heated water rises and pushes cooler water down to be warmed at the bottom of the kettle. Jupiterimages/Comstock/Thinkstock

When a fluid is heated, its density (mass per unit volume) decreases. The particles of the fluid speed up and spread out. The fluid expands, becoming more buoyant. A warmer volume of fluid will rise while a colder, and thus more compacted, volume of fluid will descend.

In a tea kettle being heated over a burner, the water in contact with the hot bottom of the kettle is heated by conduction. However,

The circulation of air by a ceiling fan is an example of forced convection. **Feng Yu/Shutterstock.com**

the heat spreads through the water by convection. The water at the bottom of the kettle becomes hotter, more energetic, and less dense than the rest of the water. Currents of the hot water rise up, pushing aside the colder water at the top of the kettle. This colder water sinks to the bottom, where it is then heated. This water then rises up, and the process is repeated. Convection transmits heat via such circulation currents of rising and descending fluid.

This process is called natural convection. Another familiar example of natural convection is the circulation of air from a hot-air furnace. When a liquid or gas is moved from one place to another by some mechanical force (rather than by differences in density), the process is known as forced convection. The circulation of air by an electric fan is an example of forced convection.

RADIATION

The third method of transferring heat from one place to another is called radiation. In radiation no material carrier transmits the energy. The source of the heat and the body that is heated are not touching, and no matter needs to move between them. A good example is the Sun radiating heat outward

This halogen space heater transfers heat through radiation. The heat it generates travels through the air until it reaches a person or object that absorbs it. **Oliver Sved/Shutterstock.com**

through the solar system. First, a heated surface (such as the Sun's) emits energy in the form of electromagnetic radiation. This radiation travels in all directions at the speed of light. Like light, it is transmitted by waves through space or even materials. Finally the radiation strikes a body where it is absorbed. The thermal energy of the body increases, and its temperature rises. When radiation from the Sun reaches the ground on Earth, the ground absorbs energy, causing its particles to speed up. Heat transferred by electromagnetic waves is known as radiant energy or thermal radiation. An electric heater transmits heat in this way.

All bodies, whether hot or cold, radiate energy. The hotter a body is, the more energy it radiates. Furthermore all bodies receive radiation from other bodies. The exchange of radiant energy goes on continuously. Thus a body at constant temperature has not stopped radiating—it is actually receiving energy at the same rate that it is radiating energy. There is no change in its thermal energy or temperature.

Heat transfer by radiation is not proportional to the difference in temperature between the hot and cold objects as it is in the case of heat transfer by conduction and convection. It is proportional to the difference between the fourth powers of the absolute temperatures (the temperatures on the Kelvin scale) of the two objects. Thus heat transfer by radiation is enormously more effective at high temperatures than at low temperatures.

Graphite is known to be a good emitter and absorber of radiation.
Andrew J. Martinez/Photo Researchers/Getty Images

Radiation transfer depends also upon the nature of the radiating object and the object that absorbs the radiation. Objects that are good emitters of thermal radiation are also good absorbers. A blackened surface is an excellent emitter as well as an excellent absorber. If the same surface is silvered, it becomes a poor emitter and a poor absorber.

CHAPTER 5

THERMODYNAMICS

T he study of the relationships between heat, other forms of energy, work, and temperature is known as thermodynamics. This branch of physics is concerned with the transfer of energy from one place to another and from one form to another. The key concept is that heat is a form of energy corresponding to a definite amount of mechanical work.

In order to apply the principles of thermo-dynamics, scientists define a system that is in some sense distinct from its surroundings. For example, the system could be a sample of gas inside a cylinder with a movable piston, an entire steam engine, a marathon runner, the planet Earth, or a black hole. In general, systems are free to exchange work, heat, and other forms of energy with their surround-ings. If a system is completely separated from its surroundings so that it can exchange nei-ther matter nor energy, it is called an isolated system. A closed system can exchange energy with its surroundings but not matter.

The internal energy of any system is the total amount of energy of the microscopic

A marathon runner can be considered a system because he can exchange matter and energy with his surroundings. Dennis Donohue/Shutterstock.com

molecules and other particles within the bodies that make up the system. It includes thermal energy (the energy of the motion of the particles) and the energy that holds the particles themselves together.

THE LAWS OF THERMODYNAMICS

The basic principles of thermodynamics are expressed in three laws. Although these laws are simple to state, they are far-reaching in their consequences.

THE FIRST LAW

The first law of thermodynamics asserts that the total amount of energy of a system plus its surroundings is conserved, or does not change. Energy can be converted into work and from one form into another, such as from kinetic energy into thermal energy. However, the amount of energy in the system stays the same. This means that the total energy of the universe remains constant. The first law expresses the law of the conservation of energy, which can be stated as "energy can be neither created nor destroyed."

According to the first law, the amount of heat that flows into a system exactly equals any change in the internal energy of the system plus all the work done by the system. This law demonstrates that adding heat to a system enables it to do work.

The movement of pistons in an engine demonstrates the first law of thermodynamics. iStockphoto/Thinkstock

The first law of thermodynamics provides a kind of strict energy accounting system, like a bank account in which the balance is changed by both withdrawals and deposits. Consider the classic example of a gas enclosed in a cylinder with a movable piston. The walls of the cylinder act as the boundary separating the gas inside from the world outside. The movable piston provides a way for the gas to do work by expanding against the force holding the piston in place. If the gas moves the piston and thus does work, it is like a withdrawal from the bank account because it reduces the energy of the gas. Some of its energy was converted into work. If heat is transferred to the gas from its surroundings through the walls of the cylinder, this adds energy and so acts like a deposit. The change in the system's internal energy will always equal the deposits (the heat added) minus the withdrawals (the work done).

THE SECOND LAW

Most kinds of energy can be changed entirely into work or other forms of energy and back again. However, heat is fundamentally different. Not all of the heat generated in a system can be changed back into work or another form of energy, not even in principle. This

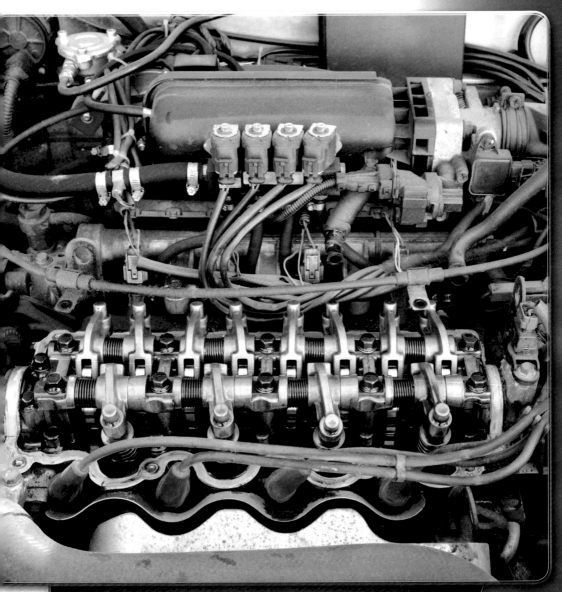

A car engine changes heat into mechanical energy and work. According to the second law of thermodynamics, however, some of the heat cannot be converted into work and is thus wasted. sima/Shutterstock.com

fundamental limitation is expressed by the second law of thermodynamics.

In a car engine, for example, hot gas expands and causes pistons to move. The mechanical energy of the pistons is then used to make the tires turn and move the car. The engine thus changes heat into mechanical energy and work. However, some of the heat simply heats up the engine and is wasted. Even if all the generated heat were collected and stored in some fashion, it could never be converted entirely back into the mechanical energy of motion. If the heat could be completely converted, the engine could be made 100 percent efficient, but unfortunately this is impossible.

A consequence of the second law is that no isolated system can spontaneously become less disordered. Thermal energy is the most disordered form of energy, since it depends on the random motions of the particles within a body. An increase in heat thus leads to an increase in the system's degree of disorder, or randomness. The measure of the amount of disorder in a system is called entropy.

THE THIRD LAW

The third law states that it is impossible for a system to actually reach absolute zero.

As the temperature of the system drops, the particles within it slow down, and their entropy decreases. Less and less thermal energy is available to be transferred from the system. As the temperature of the system approaches absolute zero, it becomes more and more difficult to extract energy from the system. Eventually, it becomes theoretically impossible.

DISCOVERING THE NATURE OF HEAT

The nature of heat has been a major subject of study since the beginnings of modern science. Some early investigators, including Galileo, Robert Boyle, and Isaac Newton, explained heat as the motion of tiny particles of which bodies are made.

THE CALORIC THEORY

In the 18th century the caloric theory of heat became widely accepted. According to this theory, heat is a fluid that flows from one object to another. The idea of a fluid to represent heat helped explain many but not all aspects of heat phenomena. Although it is now known that heat is

Antoine-Laurent Lavoisier at work. **Hulton Archive/ Getty Images**

not a material substance, the caloric theory was a step toward the present conception of energy—that is, that energy remains constant through many physical processes and transformations.

The 18th-century Scottish scientist Joseph Black distinguished heat from temperature. Both Black and the eminent French chemist Antoine-Laurent Lavoisier emphasized that changes in heat could be measured. Lavoisier developed theories that helped to explain the relations between heat and chemical reactions. However, his theories were still based on the idea that heat was a fluid.

The caloric theory remained influential until the mid-19th century. By that time many kinds of experiments forced a general recognition that heat is a form of energy transfer.

THE KINETIC THEORY AND THE DEVELOPMENT OF THERMODYNAMICS

In 1798 Benjamin Thompson (Count Rumford), a physicist and British military engineer, revived the kinetic theory of heat (which is the currently accepted one). As we have seen, this theory explains heat in terms of the kinetic energy of the particles that make up matter. Thompson became

James P. Joule. **Hulton Archive/Getty Images**

interested in the subject by observing that very high temperatures are produced when the inside of a cannon is bored, or drilled out. He noted that the amount of heat generated is proportional to the work done in turning a blunt boring tool. Thompson decided that heat is not a material fluid but a transfer of energy. His observation of the proportionality between heat generated and work done lies at the foundation of thermodynamics.

Some forty years later, the British physicist James P. Joule showed that various forms of energy—mechanical, electrical, and heat—are basically the same and can be changed into one another. He concluded that the amount of work required to bring about any given energy exchange was independent of the kind of work done, the rate of work, or the method of doing it. Therefore, in an isolated system, work can be converted into heat at a ratio of one to one. Joule thus formulated the basis of the first law of thermodynamics.

Thermodynamics developed rapidly during the 19th century in response to the need to improve the performance of steam engines. The French military engineer Sadi Carnot concerned himself with this problem. He performed research on heat that explained

Sir Benjamin Thompson

Heat was not formally recognized as a form of energy until after the investigations of the American-born British physicist Benjamin Thompson (Count Rumford), who lived from 1753 to 1814. He overturned the theory that heat is a liquid form of matter and established the beginnings of the modern theory that thermal energy is a form of motion.

During the American Revolution Thompson served as a British spy. After the war, he was forced to flee to Britain. He later entered the civil service in Bavaria (now in Germany) and became war and police minister and grand chamberlain to the ruler there. He introduced numerous social reforms and brought James Watt's steam engine into common use. His work resulted in improved fireplaces and chimneys, and among his inventions are a double boiler, a kitchen range, and a drip coffee-pot. He also introduced into Bavaria the potato as a staple food. Interest in gunpowder and weaponry stimulated his physical investigations, and in 1798 he began his studies of heat.

Benjamin Thompson, also known as Count Rumford. **Hulton Archive/Getty Images**

the mechanics of the flow of heat from a hot region to a cooler region. (However, Carnot still believed in the caloric theory of heat.) Among the other 19th-century pioneers of thermodynamics was the Scottish physicist Lord Kelvin, who used Carnot's concepts to develop an absolute temperature scale. The distinction between heat and temperature was clarified by such scientists as J.-B. Fourier of France, Gustav Kirchhoff of Germany, and Ludwig Boltzmann of Austria. The German mathematical physicist Rudolf Clausius formulated the second law of thermodynamics. By applying mathematics, Clausius, Boltzmann, and J. Willard Gibbs of the United States refined thermodynamics into an exact science.

Conclusion

As we have seen, heat is a type of energy in transition that flows from warmer substances to cooler ones. It is difficult to overstate the importance of heat. All living things need it. It is the cause of certain natural changes that occur in an endless cycle. By far the most significant source of heat for Earth is radiation from the Sun. A part of this radiation is absorbed by Earth. This keeps the temperature of Earth's surface and atmosphere at a level that permits life to continue.

The largest amount of energy is received directly below the Sun at the Equator. As one moves away from the Equator, the amount of heat received from the Sun decreases. For this reason tropical areas are warm and polar regions are cold. As a result of these temperature differences, the warm tropical air moves toward the poles, initiating a global movement, or circulation, of air. Oceans too receive differing amounts of heat. This difference results in the flow of water masses that move continuously through Earth's oceans. The study of heat transfer is thus fundamental to the study of climate and weather, as well as of biology.

In fact, the sweeping generality of the laws of thermodynamics makes them applicable to all physical and biological systems. In particular, these laws give a complete description of all changes in the energy state of any system and its ability to perform useful work on its surroundings. Scientists can use the laws of thermodynamics to study such various systems as the human heart, an airplane, a thunderstorm, Earth itself, the Milky Way, or even the entire universe.

atom The smallest particle of a chemical element that can exist either alone or in combination.

calorie A unit of energy or heat equal to the amount of heat required to raise the temperature of one gram of water from $14.5°C$ to $15.5°C$

calorimeter An apparatus for measuring quantities of absorbed or emitted heat or for determining specific heats.

conduction A point-by-point process of heat transfer within a body or between two bodies that are touching.

convection The transfer of heat by movement of a heated fluid, which can be a liquid or gas.

efficient Productive of desired effects; effective. The efficiency of a mechanical system is usually determined by the ratio of the power delivered by the system to the power supplied to it.

endothermic reaction A chemical or physical reaction in which heat is absorbed.

entropy The measure of a system's thermal energy that is unavailable for doing useful work. It is also a measure of the system's disorder, or randomness.

exothermic reaction A chemical or physical reaction in which heat is lost.

kinetic energy The energy that an object or a particle has by reason of its motion.

latent heat The amount of energy absorbed or released by a substance during a phase change (a change in its physical state) that occurs without changing its temperature.

radiation The transfer of heat by the combined processes of emission, transmission, and absorption of radiant energy.

sensible heat Thermal energy whose transfer to or from a substance results in a change of temperature but not a change in physical state.

specific heat The amount of energy required to raise a unit mass of a substance through a specified temperature interval, usually one degree.

sublimation The conversion of a substance from the solid to the vapor state without its becoming liquid.

temperature Measure of hotness or coldness expressed in terms of any of several arbitrary scales and indicating the direction in which heat energy will spontaneously flow, i.e., from a hotter body (one at a higher temperature) to a colder body (one at a lower temperature).

thermal energy The energy something has because of the motion of its particles.

thermocouple A device for measuring temperature in which a pair of wires of dissimilar metals (as copper and iron) are joined and the free ends of the wires are connected to an instrument (as a voltmeter) that measures the difference in potential created at the junction of the two metals.

thermometer An instrument for measuring temperature.

work The measure of energy transfer that occurs when an object is moved over a distance by an external force at least part of which is applied in the direction of the displacement.

American Institute of Physics (AIP)
One Physics Ellipse
College Park, MD 20740
(301) 209-3100
Web site: http://www.aip.org
The members of the AIP include scientists,
    engineers, and educators who seek to
    promote the study of physics among the
    public through programs, publications,
    and outreach services.

Canadian Association of Physicists (CAP)
Suite 112, MacDonald Building
University of Ottawa
150 Louis Pasteur Priv.
Ottawa, ON K1N 6N5
Canada
(613) 562-5614
Web site: http://www.cap.ca
Committed to advancing research and educa-
    tion in the field of physics, CAP sponsors
    meetings for physicists from throughout
    Canada, provides lectures and resources
    for students pursuing physics-related
    careers, and promotes the importance of
    physics to the public at large.

Exploratorium
3601 Lyon Street
San Francisco, CA 94123

(415) 561-0360

Web site: http://www.exploratorium.edu

Through its extensive array of interactive
exhibits and activities, the Exploratorium
fosters curiosity in physics, astronomy,
biology, and other branches of science
and nature.

Museum of Science and Industry
57th Street and Lake Shore Drive
Chicago, IL 60637
(773) 684-1414
Web site: http://www.msichicago.org

The Museum of Science and Industry is one
of the largest science museums in the
world and home to exhibits and artifacts
for visitors interested in all fields of science and technology.

National Science Foundation (NSF)
4201 Wilson Boulevard
Arlington, VA 22230
(703) 292-5111
Web site: http://www.nsf.gov

The NSF is an independent government
agency that supports scientific research
and advancement throughout the United
States in a variety of fields, including
physics and other physical sciences.

Science World at TELUS World of Science
1455 Quebec Street
Vancouver, BC V6A 3Z7
Canada
(604) 443-7443
Web site: http://www.scienceworld.ca
With interactive exhibits and educational
   programs in a variety of subject areas,
   Science World encourages the pursuit
   and enjoyment of scientific exploration
   among the public.

WEB SITES

Due to the changing nature of Internet
   links, Rosen Educational Services has
   developed an online list of Web sites
   related to the subject of this book. This
   site is updated regularly. Please use
   this link to access the list:

http://www.rosenlinks.com/inphy/heat

Bibliography

Cook, Trevor. *Experiments with Heat* (PowerKids Press, 2009).

Discovery Channel School. *Sizzle: The Heat Files* (Discovery, 2000).

Fullick, Ann. *Turning Up the Heat: Energy* (Heinemann, 2005).

Gardner, Robert, and Kemer, Eric. *Easy Genius Science Projects with Temperature and Heat* (Enslow, 2009).

Kirkland, Kyle. *Time and Thermodynamics* (Facts on File, 2007).

Lafferty, Peter. *Heat and Cold*, 3rd ed. (Times, 2000).

Saunders, Nigel, and Chapman, Steven. *Energy Transfers* (Raintree, 2006).

Snedden, Robert. *Energy Transfer*, rev. ed (Heinemann, 2007).

Whyman, Kathryn. *Energy and Heat*, new ed. (Stargazer, 2005).

Winholtz, Wallie, and others. *Thermodynamic Thrills* (Loose in the Lab, 2002).

Index